Ankylosaur Attack

A dinosaur adventure

Franklin Watts

Published in Great Britain in 2016 by The Watts Publishing Group

Published by permission of Kids Can Press Ltd, Toronto, Canada.

Edited by Valerie Wyatt
Designed by Julia Naimaska

ISBN 978 1 4451 1943 4

Dewey number: 823.9'2

Printed in China.

Franklin Watts
An imprint of
Hachette Children's Group
Part of The Watts Publishing Group
Carmelite House
50 Victoria Embankment
London EC4Y 0DZ

An Hachette UK Company

www.hachette.co.uk

www.franklinwatts.co.uk

To my brothers, James Loxton and Jason Loxton, for all the plastic dinosaur battles we had in our backyard in Metchosin, British Columbia.

ACKNOWLEDGMENTS:
Deepest thanks to Cheryl Hebert, Crystal Cerny, Andre Hebert, Daniel Abraham, Julie Roberts, Sandy Gibson, Pat Linse, David Patton, William Bull, Isaac Loxton, Desiree Schell and K.O. Myers for photographic assistance.

Special thanks to Donald Prothero, Kenneth Carpenter and Jason Loxton for expert paleontological insights. Your generosity is warmly appreciated.

Additional thanks to my colleagues Pat Linse and Michael Shermer at Skeptic magazine (www.skeptic.com) for their wisdom, support and ongoing encouragement.

Ankylosaur Attack
A dinosaur adventure

Daniel Loxton

Illustrated by Daniel Loxton
with Jim W.W. Smith

W

FRANKLIN WATTS
LONDON • SYDNEY

It was a morning long, long ago — millions of years before humans walked the Earth.

As the first rays of sunlight shone through the trees, a young ankylosaur opened his eyes. He looked around. The cool morning air began to warm up. He turned his huge armoured body to bask in the sun.

Pterosaurs circled overhead. Their huge bat-like wings caught the wind. They turned and soared.

The dinosaur watched as they squawked and screeched. He lifted his head and bellowed to the sky. But the pterosaurs paid no attention.

Birds landed on his wide back. The birds snacked on biting insects that hid between the plates of his armour. His own short legs could not reach those annoying itches. He sighed with relief.

He was hungry, too. He was already as big as a truck and still growing. He needed a lot of food.

He wandered through forest and wetland, finding
more and more food to fill his huge tummy. He ate
ferns. He ate grasses. He ate branches from the trees.

Sometimes he stopped to listen and smell the air.
He had to be careful. Fierce meat-eating dinosaurs
hunted in the wilderness. But he had strong armour to
protect him. If he had to fight, he could use the heavy
club on his tail.

But wait – what was that new smell? Could it be a meat-eater?

No. It was a dinosaur with plates of armour and a club on his tail. It was another ankylosaur!

The other dinosaur was old and big. He had scars from many battles.

The young dinosaur slowly approached the stranger. He knew that ankylosaurs mostly wanted to be left alone.

The old dinosaur was very bad tempered. He had a sore leg. The pain made him want to fight.

As the young dinosaur came near, the old one stomped the ground. He grunted and roared. He waved his tail club back and forth. The message was clear: Go away!

The young dinosaur turned to leave. He did not notice hungry eyes watching from the forest.

Peering through the branches, a fierce meat-eater watched carefully. She opened her mouth and showed her giant teeth. She drooled in hunger. She was one of the most dangerous animals in the world – a *Tyrannosaurus rex!*

The tyrannosaur saw that the old ankylosaur was injured. She waited for a chance to attack. She stood quiet and still until…

Crrraaaaash! The tyrannosaur smashed through the branches. She let out a ferocious RAAAARRRRR! Her teeth glistened. Slobber flew from her enormous mouth.

The old dinosaur turned to defend himself. His tail club was a powerful weapon. If he could swing it fast enough, he could knock the tyrannosaur off her feet. But it was too late. The meat-eater leapt at the old fighter.

The tyrannosaur chomped down on the old one's back. Giant teeth crunched and slipped over his tough plates. She bit down again and again. But her teeth could not cut through the ankylosaur's armour.

The tyrannosaur tried something new. She pushed against the old dinosaur to flip him over. If she could get him on the ground, she would bite into his soft belly.

The scarred old ankylosaur had fought many battles in his life. He had survived many dangers. But now he squealed in terror. His sore leg made him no match for a fast-moving tyrannosaur.

His body tilted as she pushed against him. Any second now, he would be on the ground. Any second now, he would be dinner for the hungry meat-eater...

Swoosh! Something heavy swung past the tyrannosaur's head. She jumped back, startled. The old ankylosaur stumbled aside.

The tyrannosaur whirled around and found herself face to face with a new enemy. It was the young ankylosaur!

Swish! Swoosh! The young ankylosaur swung his tail club from side to side. The club whooshed by, just missing the mighty meat-eater.

The young dinosaur bellowed at the tyrannosaur and kept his tail ready.

The tyrannosaur roared back. She crouched on her powerful legs. She waited for – NOW!

The tyrannosaur threw herself at the young dinosaur. But he fought back. He swung his tail as hard as he could. His club whistled through the air.

Thud! The bony club crashed into the tyrannosaur's side.

The tyrannosaur's roar turned into a yelp. She was bleeding and hurt.

She backed away. She could not win this fight. She turned and limped into the trees.

The next day, the young ankylosaur wandered and ate, wandered and ate. He was extra hungry after the fight.

Beside him, the old one ate ferns and bushes, too. Today the old dinosaur did not try to chase the young one off.

Maybe later they would go their own ways. Ankylosaurs were like that. But today, on this sunny morning, they ate peacefully, side by side.

Ankylosaurs

Ankylosaurs were plant-eating animals that lived during the age of the dinosaurs. Scientists have discovered fossils of different species of ankylosaurs in many places across our planet: in North America, South America, Asia, Europe and even Antarctica. All had short legs and wide, heavy bodies. All had tough plates of bony armour. Some had heavy clubs on their tails.

The ankylosaurs in this story are closest to *Ankylosaurus magniventris*, a species that lived in North America in areas we now call Montana, Wyoming and Alberta. They were about as long as a mid-sized truck. They roamed the lush green habitat along the coast of a shallow ancient sea, which existed where the flat grasslands called the prairies are today.

Tyrannosaurs

The meat-eating dinosaur in this story belongs to the species *Tyrannosaurus rex* – the largest and most famous of several species of tyrannosaurs found around the world. They were predators with huge heads, extra-large jaws and teeth the size and shape of bananas. They were about as long as a school bus. *Tyrannosaurus rex* shared the North American habitat of *Ankylosaurus magniventris*.

Most of the dinosaurs and flying pterosaurs in this story died out sixty-five million years ago.